Contents

Down to the sea

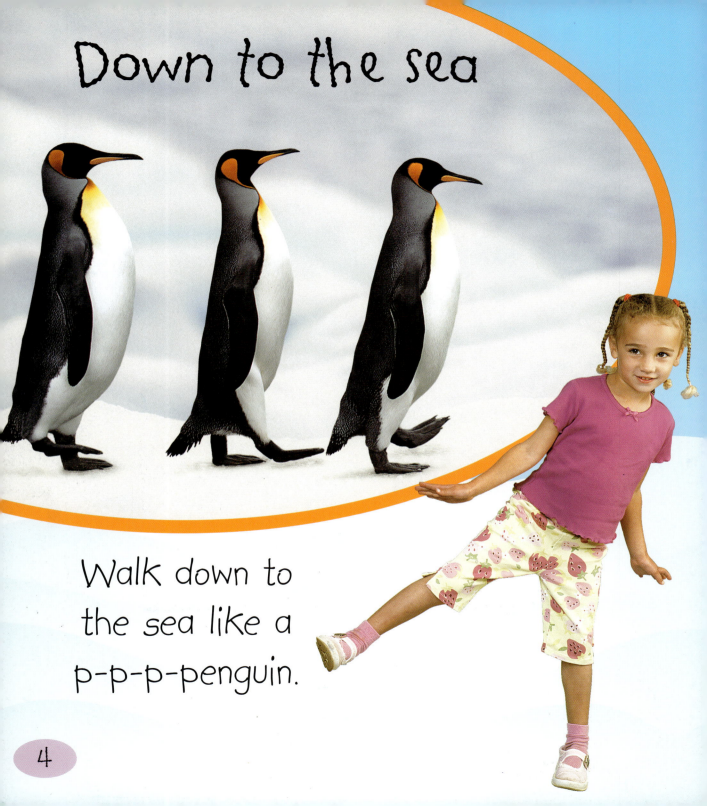

Walk down to
the sea like a
p-p-p-penguin.

Le
une ea

Heinemann
LIBRARY

Little Nippers

www.heinemann.co.uk/library
Visit our website to find out more information about **Heinemann Library** books.

To order:
☎ Phone 44 (0) 1865 888066
▤ Send a fax to 44 (0) 1865 314091
▭ Visit the Heinemann Bookshop at www.heinemann.co.uk/library to browse our catalogue and order online.

First published in Great Britain by Heinemann Library, Halley Court, Jordan Hill, Oxford OX2 8EJ, part of Harcourt Education.
Heinemann is a registered trademark of Harcourt Education Ltd.

Editorial: Jilly Attwood and Kate Bellamy
Design: Jo Hinton-Malivoire
Models made by: Jo Brooker
Picture Research: Rosie Garai and Emma Lynch
Production: Séverine Ribierre

Originated by Dot Gradations
Printed and bound in China by South China Printing Company

ISBN 0 431 16479 7 (hardback)
08 07 06 05 04
10 9 8 7 6 5 4 3 2 1

ISBN 0 431 16484 3 (paperback)
08 07 06 05 04
10 9 8 7 6 5 4 3 2 1

British Library Cataloguing in Publication Data
Lynch, Emma
Let's get moving... under the sea
591.5'09162
A full catalogue record for this book is available from the British Library.

Acknowledgements
The publishers would like to thank the following for permission to reproduce photographs: Corbis pp. **19a** (Brandon D. Cole), **7a** (Tim Davis); Corbis/Royalty Free pp. **5a, 6a, 10, 12a, 13a, 14a, 15a, 16a, 17a, 20a, 21a, 22a** (RF); Getty Images p. **4** (Digital Vision); Harcourt Education Ltd pp. **4b, 5b, 7, 9, 11, 12b, 13b, 14b, 15b, 16b, 17b, 18b, 19b, 20b, 21b, 23** (Tudor Photography); Oxford Scientific Films p. **18**.

Cover photograph reproduced with permission of Corbis/Royalty Free.

Our thanks to Annie Davy for her assistance in the preparation of this book.

Every effort has been made to contact copyright holders of any material reproduced in this book. Any omissions will be rectified in subsequent printings if notice is given to the publishers.

The paper used to print this book comes from sustainable resources.

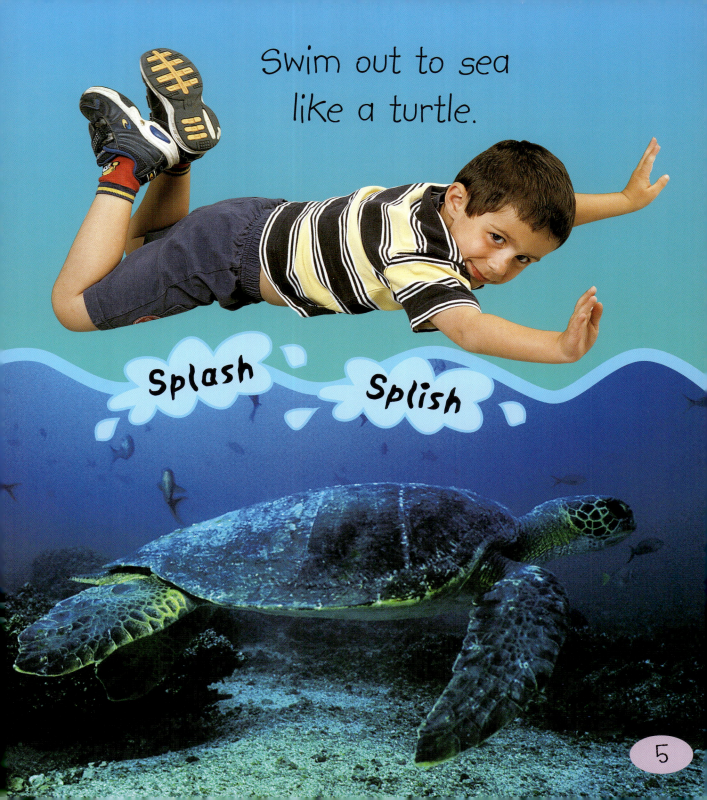

Swim out to sea
like a turtle.

Splash   Splish

In the shallows

Can you **scuttle** sideways like a crab?

scuttle

scuttle

7

Diving down

The water is very deep, so take a big breath.

Now dive
down,
down,
down
like a whale.

9

Under the sea

Swim fast like a fish.

bubble bubble whoosh!

Swim *fast.*

Swim *slow.*

Which way will you go?

11

Deep under the sea

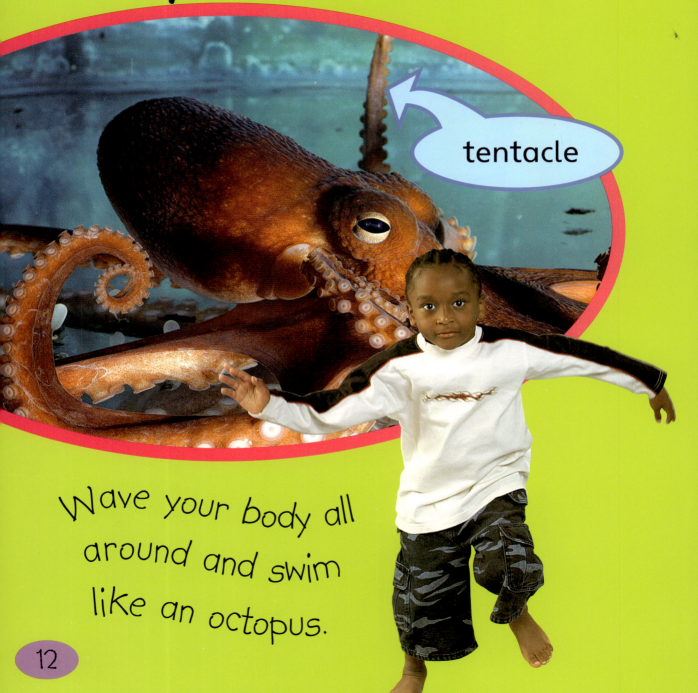

tentacle

Wave your body all around and swim like an octopus.

Twist and turn
away from a
hunting shark.

13

On the sea floor

Wave like the sea anemones.

Or **jump** and make a starfish shape.

Along the sea floor

Quietly, quietly,
glide like a ray.

16

Creep across the floor
like a sea horse.

Swimming back up

It's too quiet down here, so kick off from the bottom.

Swim like an eel towards the top.

float upwards like a jellyfish.

19

At the surface

Keep going. Keep kicking ...

... and leap up like a dolphin out of the sea.

Back on dry land

Even seals get tired, so swim ashore and have a rest.

Come back soon for
more underwater fun!

Index

The end

Notes for adults

Let's get moving! explores the many different ways humans can move and encourages children to take part in physical activity. *Let's get moving!* also supports children's growing knowledge and understanding of the wider world, introducing them to different plants and animals and the way they move and grow. Used together, the books will enable comparison of different movements and of a variety of habitats and the animals that live in them.

The key curriculum Early Learning Goals relevant to this series are:

Early Learning Goals for movement
- Move with confidence, imagination and in safety
- Move with control and coordination

Early Learning Goals for sense of space
- Show awareness of space, self and of others

Early Learning Goals for exploration and investigation
- Find out about and identify some features of living things

This book introduces the reader to a range of movements used by animals under the sea. It will also help children extend their vocabulary as they hear new words like *tentacle, anemone* and *scuttle*. You may like to introduce and explain other new words yourself, like *shoal, habitat* and *ocean*.

Additional information

Most living things can move. Humans and many other animals have skeletons and muscles to support and protect their bodies and to help them move. About 71% of the Earth's surface is covered by oceans, seas, gulfs and straits. The Pacific Ocean is the largest. It covers almost one third of the Earth's area. Millions of plants and animals live in the world's seas and oceans. Some are yet to be discovered.

Follow-up activities
- Can the children think of other sea creatures? Try to copy their movements.
- Think of some other habitats in your local area (e.g. field, wood, river, pond). Which animals live there and how do they move?
- Learn and sing an action song about the body, like 'Heads, Shoulders, Knees and Toes'. Think about how each part of the body can move.

CAPTAIN GREEN
AND THE TREE MACHINE

Written by Evelyn Bookless   Illustrated by Danny Deeptown

Marshall Cavendish Children

For Cillian, and all lovers of living things

~ E.B.

For Nanny Dando, you were the first to teach me to nurture nature

~ D.D.

KLONK! CLASH! CLANG!

Captain Green, the Caped Captain of Clean, worked on a superhero invention to protect the planet. "One day my Green Machine will…"

"Hmmm…?"

BRRNG! Captain Green's watch rang.

"Duty calls! I've got to go."

On a far-off island, Hornbill squawked. "Help! My nesting tree has been chopped down. I must protect my eggs."

"Do not fear, the Captain is here."

Captain Green searched long and hard to find a new home for Hornbill.

"Thank you," said Hornbill.
"My chicks will be safe here."

"Happy to help," said Captain Green
and off he flew.

BRRNG!

GURGLE! GRUMBLE! GROWL!

Elephant's tummy groaned.
Trucks raced off with her fruit and
leaves. There was nothing left to eat!

"Do not fear, the Captain is here!"

Captain Green gazed
as far as he could see.

"Trees to the east," he said.
"Follow me."

"Food at last! Thank you,"
said Elephant.

Time to get back to my Green Machine, thought Captain Green.

BRRNG!

Oh, no! Fires blazed in Orangutan's forest.

"Do not fear, the Captain is here!"
Captain Green swooped down, grabbed Orangutan and zoomed up high.
"ACK!" They coughed and choked on the smoky air.

"Here you go little fella," said Captain Green.

"You saved me," said Orangutan.
"But my home has turned to ash."

"Don't worry, I'll find a way to fix your forest!"
said Captain Green.

But Captain Green's tummy tightened.
How could he replace so many trees?

Captain Green dashed back to his workshop.

I know! I will use my invention to grow new trees!

SMASH!
WHACK!
WHUMP!

TA-DA!

A TREE
MACHINE!

"Finally, a gadget fit
for a superhero!"

"I hope this works!" said Captain Green.

ZAAAP!

A tree flew out, planted in the ground and stretched up toward the sky.

"Phew! But I'll need to go faster."

Captain Green activated MAX Plant.

ZAAAAP!

ZOOOP!

Trees sprang up all around.

Orangutan cheered and leapt from branch to branch. "I can swing again!"

"Green-tastic!" said Captain Green,
"but there's still lots to do!"

Captain Green tried to fix his Tree Machine, but it was no use.
"It seems easier to ruin a forest, than to grow one!"

Captain Green slumped. *How will I save the animals now?*

Then, as he headed home, he spotted something truly super. **"OF COURSE!"** he said. "I don't have to do this on my own."

He knew just where to go.

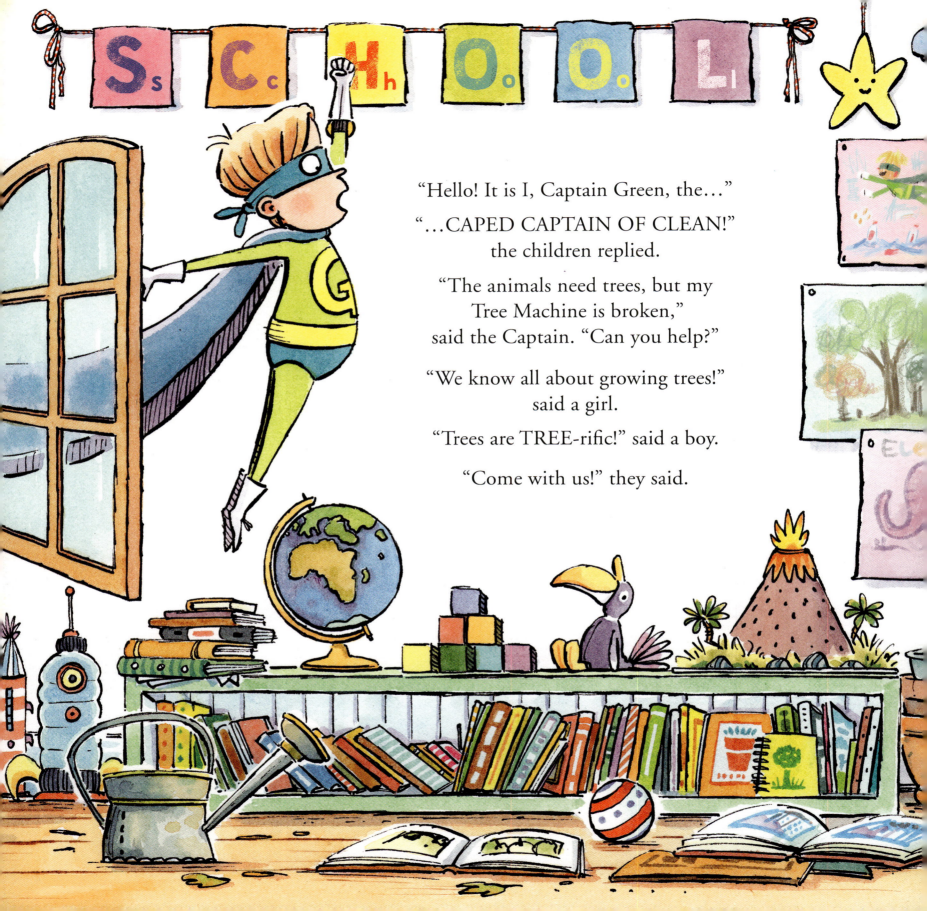

"Hello! It is I, Captain Green, the…"

"…CAPED CAPTAIN OF CLEAN!"
the children replied.

"The animals need trees, but my
Tree Machine is broken,"
said the Captain. "Can you help?"

"We know all about growing trees!"
said a girl.

"Trees are TREE-rific!" said a boy.

"Come with us!" they said.

"My green-ness, this is fun!" said Captain Green.
"If everyone plants a tree or two, the planet can grow green again."

"We promise to plant lots of trees!" said a girl.

"You all can be my Tree Machine!" said Captain Green.

Everyone cheered.

"TREE-mendous!" said Captain Green.

Then off he flew to spread the word.

WHOOSH!

"Remember now,
you don't need superpowers
to save the animals.
Together we can…"

"KEEP IT GREEN!"

Captain Green's Green Facts

Eighty per cent of all plants, insects and animals live in forests. This makes forests one of the most important ecosystems on earth. An ecosystem is an area where plants, animals and insects live and depend on one another to survive. But ecosystems are destroyed when trees and forests are cut down for things that humans want, such as paper, furniture and wood, or burned for farmland to grow crops.

Trees are like the Earth's superheroes. Just like Captain Green, they work hard to help our planet. They help to keep the climate cool, filter water through their roots, and create the air we breathe by absorbing a gas called carbon dioxide and making oxygen.

Some animals are endangered which means they are at risk of becoming extinct or not being alive anymore. Hornbills, pygmy elephants and orangutans live in South East Asia. Like many other animals all around the world, they are losing the ecosystems that are their homes and food sources. Just like humans, all animals need food to eat and a safe place to sleep.

Help Save the Forests!

- Use recycled paper and cardboard for drawing and painting. Write on both sides and then recycle it again when you're finished!

- Ask your parents to buy foods like bananas, chocolate and coffee that are grown in a sustainable way. That means they are safe for the environment, for wildlife, and for people.

- Enormous areas of rainforest are cleared each year to make room to grow the palm trees that produce palm oil. Ask your parents to read the labels when shopping for food and toiletries to check that any palm oil in them is from a sustainable source. This means they are farmed in a way that does not harm the planet.

- Eat less meat. Lots of forests are cut down just to make space to farm animals for people to eat.

- Avoid wasting food. By only producing the food we need, we save land, water and energy.

- Plant a tree or two! Trees take years to mature – measure yourself growing alongside them!

SPREAD THE WORD! LET'S KEEP IT GREEN TOGETHER!

Published by Marshall Cavendish Children
An imprint of Marshall Cavendish International

A member of the
Times Publishing Group

Other Marshall Cavendish Offices:
Marshall Cavendish Corporation, 800 Westchester Ave, Suite N-641, Rye Brook,
NY 10573, USA • Marshall Cavendish International (Thailand) Co Ltd, 253 Asoke,
16th Floor, Sukhumvit 21 Road, Klongtoey Nua, Wattana, Bangkok 10110, Thailand
• Marshall Cavendish (Malaysia) Sdn Bhd, Times Subang, Lot 46, Subang Hi-Tech
Industrial Park, Batu Tiga, 40000 Shah Alam, Selangor Darul Ehsan, Malaysia

Marshall Cavendish is a registered trademark of Times Publishing Limited

National Library Board, Singapore Cataloguing in Publication Data

Name(s): Evelyn Bookless. | Deeptown, Danny, illustrator.
Title: Captain Green and the tree machine / written by Evelyn Bookless ;
illustrated by Danny Deeptown.
Description: Singapore : Marshall Cavendish Children, [2020]
Identifier(s): OCN 1163606633 | ISBN 978-981-48-9320-6
Subject(s): LCSH: Deforestation--Juvenile fiction. | Forest conservation--Juvenile fiction.
Classification: DDC 428.6--dc23

Printed in Singapore

*"A beautiful, informative way to educate
the next generation about the importance of
ending deforestation. Children of today are
our future, and books like this will help inspire
them to protect our world and its species."*

Rainforest Trust

*"Captain Green and the Tree Machine is
an engaging story for young children who
learn that trees are truly superheroes.
This is a great way to inspire children
and families to join together to protect
and restore the world's forests."*

WeForest

*"A very sweet and important story that
not only helps kids understand the impact of
deforestation on wildlife, but also the power
of making a positive difference when
we come together for sustainability."*

Diana Chaplin, Canopy Director, One Tree Planted